Her Breath on the Window

Books by Karenmaria Subach

Mysteries
Her Breath on the Window

Her Breath on the Window

Karenmaria Subach

Carnegie Mellon University Press
Pittsburgh 2024

Acknowledgments

The American Poetry Review: "Ars Poetica" ("In the pond of the Palazzo Medici . . ."),
    "Rabbits at Iraklion"
Birmingham Poetry Review: "At the Raptor Center," "Saul, Changed"
The Classical Quarterly: "Procne"
CutBank: "Tattoo"
Folio: "Her Breath on the Window"
The Georgetown Review: "Whatever the White Mountain Means"
Iowa Journal of Literary Studies: "The Kyria's Tuesday Vigil"
Kalliope: "In the Baths, in Budapest," "Veronica and the Strange Cloth"
The Laurel Review: "Melancholia: Five Movements"
Orphic Lute: "Cleopatra at the Mirror"
Pleiades: "Tuesday the Conductor Travels," "Ars Poetica" ("The wild green man . . .")
Pudding: "In the Cottage of the Dwarfs"
Without Halos: "Peace with the Wolf"

"A Long Story," "Saul, Changed," and "Veronica and the Strange Cloth" appeared in my
chapbook, *Mysteries*, Finishing Line Press, 2009.

"Tattoo" appeared in *The Chance of a Ghost*, eds. Gloria Vando and Philip Miller, Helicon
Nine Editions, 2005.

"Ars Poetica" ("The wild green man . . .") appeared in *Poets and the Fools Who Love Them*, by
Richard Katrovas, Louisiana State University Press, 2022.

"At the Raptor Center" was part of Nancy Prawdzik's multimedia Bird Box for the Tubac
Center of the Arts Public Walkways Project in Tucson, spring, 2015.

The Thouron Foundation of the University of Pennsylvania, the English Department of
Princeton University, the German Academic Exchange Service (D.A.A.D.), and the Iowa
Writer's Workshop provided significant opportunities and graduate fellowships, as did the
Corporation of Yaddo, Washburn University of Topeka, the Sewanee Writers' Conference,
the Bread Loaf Writers' Conference, and Shirley Vonderhaar, Director of the James E.
Kennedy Library, through the NEH *Poets in Person* series. The creative legerdemain and
warm leadership of Amy Margolis, Director of the Iowa Summer Writing Festival; Peggy
Houston, Founding Director of the ISWF; and Kelly Flinn, Director of the University
of Iowa Center for Conferences, have been sustaining, as has been the Prague Summer
Program for Writers. Jacki Laird (Miss Wysocki). Barbara A. Geary Truan. David
Bernstein, MD. Dr. Margaret Soenser Breen. Dr. Constance Harsh. LFG. BB. JB. RGL.
BV. All cherished others within my beloved family of friends: thank you. And to my family,
especially Alice Ursula Marks, Tati Alicija: *ačiu labai* and *dziękuję*.

Book designed by Jennifer Bortner

In memoriam

> *Michael D. Kenig (1942–2021)*
> *esteemed teacher—*

and for Wayne Johnson
and Richard Katrovas
with love and gratitude

Contents

Beyond all faces there is one face,
but this does not mean that each one's face is not his own.

—Jane Roberts

Du schnell vergehendes Daguerreotyp
in meinen langsamer vergehenden Händen.

You quickly fading daguerreotype
in my more slowly fading hands.

—Rainer Maria Rilke
"Jugendbildnis meines Vaters"

I. *The Beautiful Apple*

Ars Poetica

In the pond of the Palazzo Medici
young Lorenzo is sailing a vellum boat
inscribed with Ptolemaic geometry.
He does not know what he cut from the tome lying open.
He just wanted a boat.

In the largest room of the stone palace
that faces the pond,
the seventeen-year-old Sandro Botticelli
is grinding paint in the billowing light,
mixing the thick oils; making the same face—
Virgin and Aphrodite—
because Love is one holiness combined.
He paints the sighs again,

for which Lorenzo, much later, will find himself writing

    ne gli occhi hanno altro lume che l'obietto

of the lover;
and

    poi ch'io gustai . . . la tua dolcezza

of Jesus.

It is 1461; the ink on the vellum blurs,
and Lorenzo feels he loves this, feels suddenly
the blurring hand of the Egyptian who marked it,
wants with his heart to think,
It's just the wind, running,
running from the dark pond.

The Kyria's Tuesday Vigil

Kyria Bellissi, bent, horn-handed,
encroaches, black-clothed, for our sheets—
eyes our hands (no gold bands)
and sighs, sly-browed. What to say? Discreet
Kyria's Greek is Peloponnesian;
ours, BBC—we can offer her tea.
Mint, she insists. Her forebears, Ephesian.
Won't sit, sips quickly, limps off to the sea,
orthopedically: her dominion,
where to summon Poseidon unstiffens; charms.
It's what she comes for, bent-winged and
pinioned in aloes, keening toward him. She
alarms us, unclothed roan squat Kyria out there
teal-sheeted with him. Bright foam. White wild hair.

Riddles

after the Anglo-Saxon

I.

The wingèd ones would nest with part of me
but do not know
my shining teeth
are just old bone.
Tell now my name.

(Comb)

II.

Of all, I am the richest!
Everything I see I own.
When you come close,
do so with care,
for I can swallow you.
You would not know.
See, you cannot see me.
Tell, if you are wise, my name.

(Mirror)

III.

Forsooth, this hall of ale has met me merrily,
although I am much used; much worn.
The maids are glad to see me
in hand of woman wise,
though those long wed will start a bit
and spill their mead—
for I am a swiving beast.
Tell what else I am.

(Knave of Hearts)

IV.

From kin of shapeshifters I come.
Three kingdoms are mine,
and I am home to man, beast; fowl—
though, too, the killer meets his end in me.
What am I?

(Tree)

At the Raptor Center

The dun hoot owl with hammered gold eyes
lifted his sandy foot,
knew too much—
sooth hieroglyph
unloosed from ancient tomb—

was not susceptible to curiosity,
remembered the desert crossing
and the bleached bones,

had tasted the braceleted arms of children,
pinned six onyx clasps
from the braids of Nubian maidens
under his wings,
spun his head once,
was mute,
refused three peeled rats
from his high perch,

would not tell of Hadrian's sweet Antinöus,
whom he knew to have washed up near Dairut,
having struggled and expired,
knifed on a Nile barge
by the trembling hierodule;

believed in the secret beesting,
the three elixirs of forgetfulness,
the blue obelisk;
had known the stone speech of the Sphinx,
and that her eye moved—

would not guarantee my safe passage,
made no shadow, I saw,
and did not breathe.

Cleopatra at the Mirror

Free, madam, no! I made no such report.
He's bound unto Octavia.

   —Antony and Cleopatra, Act II, Scene 5

Tell me: is she fair?
I would know all he said.
And the color of her hair.

This month again the pale moon pares
my heart. Apart, does he stand? Sit? Dread
mars me: I pale that she should be fair.

In sleep again I'll sail the Cydnus. Spare
me, mandragora, this empty bed.
Let me see it. That color. Her hair.

I pale, Charmian. Cut my lace. Bear
me up with flutes and blue herbs for my head.
Smooth pillows against her fairer

face. In dreams my Love's halved face declares
unto this Other. Love, I'm full of lead,
but name it: the fairer-haired—

who? Worm of Nilus, quick kill that drains not,
where is the draught of potion that pains not?
Give it here, quickly. I pale.
   And still would know: is she fairest?
As well the color. Her hair.

In the Cottage of the Dwarfs

Snow White longed for the beautiful apple.

"Against all warning I shall take—
just half."

She wants all of it but is well-bred. She's
named the graspable part.

How close this fruit has come to complete. She
winces as the queen cuts it.

Remember that the apple is poisoned,
but she cannot know this.

She would not want it if it were not perfect.

She is tied to the queen now
because the apple looks perfect,
even if the apple offered and the apple taken
are two separate fruits.

How can she know
she is taking a bite of the queen
in choosing? In wanting? In being about to eat?

Although her wanting differs from the wanting of the queen,
being pure:
       she does not know yet
       that some things she will not have.

She must have this.
There is nothing to decide.

She reaches for it because no one has touched her.

How can she have been so stupid,
the dwarf who finds her will ask himself, washing
her with wine;
building the glass coffin.

Waste, waste, all that loveliness—

he will be furious because he cannot know
that what some women feared was this kind of beauty,
which was illusion yet power in the world of men.

II. *Anaconda and Magenta Bird*

Whose hand carries the ball?
Probably the Son's.
And the whole earth is in it—
Paradise and Hell.

—Czesław Miłosz
"The Garden of Earthly Delights"

From Bourbonnais

Anno Domini 1151

I am called Georges Lamar de Payens,
and I come from the Holy Wars,
finally at Nicholastide,
my bones feeling the cold
of Saint-Amand-Montrond
for the first winter of my life
although I am not old.

Tomorrow the butchered stag
will be served on heavy plates
in the duke's great hall,
and only three of us who marched
with flags waving, winters end,
three ago, will eat.
Jean-Michel and Guillaume, my cousins,
will carve, and I will offer grace.
In all our lives we have never been so honored.

Snow blowing over this rooftop reminds me of sifting sand,
and I am weeping.
I do not know what to do in this silence.

My father has bid me keep to my bed and be served, but
in my sleep there are the maiden's brown hands, rubbed
with almond oil—
the magenta silk veil blowing from her face.
She has your eyes, and I must find her.

Near Damascus I traded the jesses of a palace falcon
for a blue perfume flask with a gold band.
I am not sure for what reason.

It was just after our regiment dismembered a boy,
who had survived, albeit wounded,
and I turned in the dust and uproar
and dug my hands into my thighs
and called to you.

The boy's skin was the color of hazelnuts and the local tea.
His hair was so thick! Of course
they beheaded him,
as along the way we had found the remains of our own
picked over by animals.

It is not that I am ungrateful for my life,
but that what I recall
causes me to doubt my ability to continue
as a man in this kingdom.

The first Saracen who fell at my hands
carried a carved box that contained
powders and a tied scroll.

These I traded for a dressed lamb
that a good woman cooked for me.
Most of it I ate in two meals.
The rest I tied under my horse to dry.

They were far better horsemen,
but we believed that our only hope for paradise
was by the sword,
and so in the name of Christ Crucified
fought until the end.

In my fury I longed for church bells
and wagons on the cobbled road to my father's house,
my hawks circling above.

Our leader violated the only daughter of a sultan
and was cut to pieces,
his testicles thrown to street dogs.

When I could sleep again, it was on a boat
from Crete to my own sweet France.
My side had been stitched.
They had given me a liquor made from dates
and mixed with one crushed pearl,
for which Guillaume had traded his mother's rosary.

I violated no woman.

One thing I did take was a tile chip from a ruined minaret,
and sometimes I put it in my mouth.

If I do not take a wife,
I must swear my life to Christ,
serving the abbot.
I feel I have paid enough.

Even the Imam of Shahbah boiled oil against us
and rushed with his glistening sword
until we finished him.
I wish
we had not taken apart his face.

My enemies recited lines that were like chanting,
but I cannot say what the holy books hold
in the stone turret that I touch, leaning out.

I have been told that the brothers of the abbey
are seasoning goose fat for their Christmas loaves
and will see six village girls suckling by harvest.

So I shall marry Marie-Claire,
cousin to my cousin,
and grow old, I pray, in peace,
dear Giles.

I will know when this reaches your own England.
My heart will tell me.
Always it will be too long
since we have spoken.
God keep you.

Night Prayers

I'm stringing these beads to temper a tantrum:
the span of my mantra of Marys
may spare me. Sister said. (*Answer*, you can please—) Frantic,
I'm yes. O Blue Cape, Smooth-footed, rant rant I'm buried
again, gone under: the gang's here again, accustomed to
    costume.
I stomached Auntie's primpings. Red-heeled She! Lipsticked
    the guests in,
and, liquory, snapped my switch off. Barbi went she-Beelzy,
    bossed
me to Lucifer, redly sprung from cat: growly/a-fester,
fleshless but be-clawed, and Drool, he's eating my shoes again:
    he's started with my shoes.
Goodnesses, Serpent Crusher, Mystical Star of the Seas,
say now what to do:
here's taily Seraphina the Mathnun peeling peeling
my ankle, yum-squeal, now Beelzy is bright is looming.
That Clover was crimped to diminish the Bigness of Blooming.

I know now: Saint Patrick saw—*G-d* is too big.

Just get here.

In the Attic

*O young girl, throw yourself into the water again
so that I may, a second time, have the chance
of saving both of us.*
　　　　　　—Albert Camus, *The Fall*

I.

At first he was staid; intent.
Like he was when you met him.

He fell down finally, clown-like, dashing though,
and the *koruny* bounced out of his pockets
and rolled into the corners.

Then raving like a kookaburra,
loose in his family's house, hands shaking:

　　　Hol' mir die Flasche ein!

We are in the attic.
So many books and maps.
I propped him up; poured the kvass—
in Prague we'd sat talking,
we'd gone to sleep, gone walking,
he watched his feet, twisted his fingers,
inspected the scars on his palms;
never asked for anything
or about Eva even or me—wanted just to know
how much it cost, signing the forms.

I know, I know, but I did it anyway.

And so drove through snowdrifts
with him in tow, Bavaria to Bohemia,

he wanted it: to go to another country;
to pull himself up; eat a meal
in Franz Kafka's back garden.

II.

Kannst Du aber spüren, he went on,
wie ich Dich liebe? Brightening, gesturing,
knocking over ashtrays, a figurine;
the carafe.

Midnight it was snowing.
From an étagère he lifted a pouch,
took out the pewter comb I'd given back.
I slid into a chair and watched candles
throwing phantoms, alligators; angels
across the ceiling.

He asked for a pen and paper—was stumbling
around:

> *Ob Du mich liebst?*
> *Ob Du mich noch liebst?*

Okay, I shouldn't have, but I told him *Ohne Zweifel*.
You've said I've "got this thing" for pretty men.

He set my comb in the basin of a washstand,
lifted a pitcher, poured water,
smeared soap across his face, looked over,
and laughed.
A squirrel ran across the roof gables.

From a drawer he lifted a horn-handled blade.
He turned to the dark panes, and shouted,

Schau' mal aus dem Fenster hinaus!

Lapsed into dialect, called

Nietzsche! Novalis!

then

*La terre est obscure, chère amoure
le bois épais, opaque le linceul!*

III.

He reached under a green mohair sofa;
dragged out a black case;
blistered leather; trapezoid.
Then opened it.

He looked up, grinned, and pounded the floor.
He laughed with his head back, mouth wide open,
two gold teeth,
uneven mustache, chocolate on his chin,
raspberry on his sleeve.
He looked down at the red velvet lining.
Across the inside of the lid were gray streaks—
the impressions of strings.
He lifted the zither as though he were picking up Eva.
We passed the house where she lives now.
I couldn't say a word.

He put his cheek to the instrument,
the smooth back; the curves.
He zigzagged a hell strain, then was crying.
I dropped my glass.

IV.

Then he scribbled some notes on paper.
Foxes on the edge of the park were raving.
It was dark. I found another candle.

Slanted beams, cedar closets; chifforobes—
the shadow shapes of wrapped statues;
of lamps.

He sat writing.
I poured cognac.
It kept snowing, and wind ripped the chimes
from the eaves of the little terrace outside this window
and dashed them against the glass.

He said, "Here, play here something,"
and pushed the zither toward me.

    Hol' mir die Flasche! More light!

He looked into a greenish mirror on the floor;
wiped shaving cream from the glass with his bare hand—
He called me *Blauestes Röschen,*
then picked up his razor and scraped at his face.

He fumbled for something in his pocket;
found a blue phial,
tapped it against the mirror.

Holderlin, Heine, he recited them,
stupefied; beautifully.
He tapped his foot to the meter of

> *Für Dich, für Dich,*
> *Es hat mein Herz für Dich geschlagen—*

Muslin knight's shirt, embroidered pants,
I nearly forgot to write what he was wearing—
I went to get my pen to start this but first
mauled him on the Persian carpet.

V.

O, correlative for Beauty
O, numenal
Your wildness is magnificent—I thought and would have said;
and feel he felt there, cutting another line, blood on the razor—

I said this to him years ago
in the English Garden.
It was his first English lesson, so to say.
We were naked,
throwing a Frisbee.
I sent you a postcard.
Before the one from Vienna.

You have always been right about this:
everything outside me at times feels bound
in the exquisite bones of his face.

Once in a glade of the Hofgarten,
his mother, the sculptress,
smoothed clay across my face
and made a terra-cotta mask.
In Magritte's *Gigantesques* the woman keeps peeling
and peeling the superimposed rapist away,
and this is how it is,
the shadow-cast of him through which I've tried to move.
Remember, he pushed a lit cigar end into his palm
(or maybe I meant to tell you this),
—to see how much he could take,
or to see how much I could.

VI.

I just rolled over and am thinking that I cannot save him.
I've embroidered a little rose on his cuff.
He's out cold. It's five a.m.

What haven't I told you?
I agree with his *copain*, Camus—Have I told you he told me
they were drinking buddies?
"Debauchery confers immortality," and I am
watching, watching
his eyelids moving in deep dream sleep, how
he soars in bliss, is liberated, suffers
no obligations, possesses only himself,
no past, no future, no promises,

no penalty, he leaves behind
all fear and all hope.
The truth of him is this: snoring now; drooling.
Oh, and he pissed in the humidor.

You told me before I came here that things don't change.
I had to come anyway.
I've just pulled off his boots.
He's divine, though, really, still familiar;
please don't laugh, don't laugh.
This is about my trying to live again in the world.

They're coming for him the day after tomorrow.
I could push my needle right through his heart,
I could, and you know why:
I love him like I love myself.
Postlapsaria, this, then, you've told me, here it is,
X. still warm against me on the floor,
and I no better than Clemence. You've read *La Chute*?
Anyway, Happy New Year, dearest Meredith!
I'd be gone by the time they found him.

Peace with the Wolf

At first cut the huntsman saw the little red cloak.

They didn't have to slit him so.
Inside it became warmth; a return:
he swallowed me whole, but I wasn't devoured.

I drowsed, and the heartbeat took me back.
It was very dark, but I could hear the commotion
when they entered the little room
beyond the wolf's snore.

If Oma had stayed dead, all would be different.
I could never speak again,
for it happened that each time
I picked her a flower along the way,
I saw another prettier one farther—
and so went deeper into the forest,
and he arrived at her door before me.

She sugars her cookies in the kitchen.
She needs me nearby
because we were in the same belly.

The huntsman took the pelt.
I could not face it.
No matter what, at one time
it was so warm; gray and lovely—

which then they weighted with my beautiful stones.

Her Breath on the Window

Manaus, Brazil: 1907

Along green parts of the Amazon is a tree,
and in the tree the fruit breathes
river mist and songs of birds.
The woman in the city eats of this tree and the silver
that *is its singing.* She leans out her wet window
in the tropical rain. She licks her pen.

Her page is wet; her hand sticky. She has a pen
pal, so to say, in France, where now trees
shake down their burnished leaves, and windows
fog with the steaming breath
of a tea table set with silver
and Aghabani; the bird-

shaped salt and pepper shakers *in a place of civilized birds.*
So far. So dull. *Were there a way,* she has written, and her pen
lies in its wish and waits to commit more. Silver
rain spatters every budding tree
along her avenue. Her breath
is fruity. She *loves guava!* She *loves Brazil,* and from her
    window

wants not to be calling to walls of windows:
to the atelier a world away that fills with leaves and bird
droppings. The one who lost his breath
writing her to come to Valence has penned
his last lines before leaving. The trees
along the Rhône sadden him. His hair is silver,

and the diamond in his pocket is set in silver
for the image she was at the window

when last he saw her waving. A painting of a tree
was the last he did in France. *Anaconda and Magenta Bird*
he named it *to show coexistence; resignation.* Pensive,
he packed canvas, pigment, paper; wood. He breathes

easily now, having booked passage. Breath
comes easily too to the woman whose silver
wishes have fallen like rain through her pen:
because; what if—. From the ledge of her window
she is answering him, his bird-
in-Brazil. They will marry *under an Amazon tree*

and its fruit. Now her breath on the window
silvers the singing bird
that flies from her pen to the tree.

Whatever the White Mountain Means

All Hallows, and a dead bride, nine, runs off
in Goodwill taffeta through spinning yellow leaves.
"I'm dead!" she shrieks. Her train is blown aloft.
"Fly!" cries a genie.

Wind weaves the crêpe of blown witch legs
into spider shapes—makes pumpkins flicker.
Twilight shimmers blue to black, then capes
the Wasatch to Sasquatch. *Boo!* Snickers;

Kit Kats. Late treaters maraud with bobbing torches.
A sudden snow at midnight eats the moon.
Cat paw prints now along the rails of porches.
Wicks sputter out, and soon

the saints—or souls—such kites
as fly like brides take shape
in maple leaves outlined in frost of sidewalks.
On glass a breath-kiss fades. But whose?
What message, pray,

in sudden snow, or whirled torn hems
of a bride's dead gown, just sold for fifty cents
at Halloween?—In genie-steam calligraphy
above my morning cup: *hello*—

A glimpse of Isabelle singing over her sewing:
twelve years. What slips through has traveled far
to come so wished-for.

I have to think of flight and gowns of snow
as part of whatever causes us to summon them.

Songs, stitched in kisses forever.

Whatever part of mending
the sudden white of this mountain means.

III. *A Box of Cedar*

Melancholia: Five Movements

I.

In this place whose language
is not yet my own,
a soldier with my brother's face
leaves a bunch of violets quietly
next to my saucer.

What is his name?
All of the missings, falling, falling,
and the leaves falling on the tables
in the central square of Kraków,
where I write among the living.

II.

Evening and the empty cafe and my open book.
A prostitute eats her mashed potatoes and gravy
with her dirty gloves on.

III.

A poet in his eighties,
walking stiffly in a square,
unfolds a faded clipping from his wallet:
The Manchester Guardian.
His son Simcha, a physicist,
born exactly a year after the war,
in celebration,
has named a kind of star.

"This is why you must have a baby!" the man says.
Blue eyes, blue tattoo,
in the camps he became a poet,
taking his watch apart over and over;
putting it back together
to bind a metaphor.
"But you must read Polish!" he says.
"It looks so nice on your mouth."

IV.

In the pastures below Suwałki,
where the grandfather of my grandmother
sang harvest songs I've heard in dialect
and played fiddle "to make the angels weep,"
I am looking through the simple gravestones.
None for the ones who disappeared—

my cousins, look-alikes, I'm told,
with my eyes—a painter and a schoolteacher—
taken into a barn when the Germans came through—
who hardly spoke again but painted and drew—

V.

Just before dark
the horses come, pulling the wagons of flowers.
In the rain, in the square,
candles in little glasses
on wet cobblestone.

When I offer my armful of yellow roses
to the nuns who are letting me stay,
they say *Für die Mutter Gottes*,
and point to Our Lady of Częstochowa
with the sword slash through her face.

Veronica and the Strange Cloth

I wanted him to take it;
to have one last thing to keep,
but he gave it back.

I was embarrassed;
strangely rejected.
My head veil,
handed back with blood on it,
my veil that Yakov's mother had woven.

Everyone looked at me: a betrothed girl with loose hair!
I rushed home with my hair down
and wept when I shut the door.

They thought I'd been with Yakov.
They would not look at me until I gathered my wits
and, shaking, could show them.

I must tell you I did not see the face at first.
I was weeping out of anguish for the dark man with the
beautiful eyes.

My mother heated water immediately—

> *an accident near the market!*

She added salt and fat.
I watched her throw the cloth in
and turn it with a laundering beam.

When she wrung it,
she called my father.
They hung it inside because
in the courtyard what would be said?

My father looked at me strangely ever after.
He thought to burn the thing,
but my mother felt that something might be true:
a message *for her.*

That such should come to a daughter of hers
she could hardly believe.

She owned it then;
I never saw it after;
I could not ask—

And so she folded it with sprigs of mint and oregano
and put it into a box of cedar.

Ars Poetica

I. The wild green man chased himself around a tree,
    crying,

> "The green man chased a wild crying tree!
> The tree chased a wild man and cried,
> 'Green!'"

II. The green of one wild tree turned the man into
     a crying man.

III. Truly I heard in the wild green the crying
      both of men and trees.

The Informant

Dollars, passports, driver; gun—
Popov paces late, planning.
Tastes the train to Warsaw, to Berlin; suns
in imagined Miami. He scans
trams, cafes, and parks; the stairwells on his list—
clicks the incriminating exchange. *Good!*
belches the official. But Popov knows *slipped*
is the word entered. And starts in his bed. Should
he live in Venice Beach or Beverly Hills; eat steak
or take up vegetarianism? No snow!
No lines. *If only* is Popov's prayer. Most things are traded
anyway. He wires a dissident's toilet; smokes.
Is lonely, kissing, kissing
his compensation. Too bad for X (and Y and Z),
stamped, at headquarters, "Missing."

Tuesday the Conductor Travels

Over Greenland a dream of cacophony
uncurls in his throat:
his symphony on fire!
Six measures expire—
singe his tongue black—
lit ghosts; loose ash—

The conductor is choking in his sleep,
and passengers are distracted.

"Music is burning!" he cries.
Rips at his cravat;
strains against the seat belt; is bolted.
Sees a stewardess smooth her uniform,
returning.

> *Vienna's crowded halls, mirrored walls—*
> *applause, applause; roses—*

Now flushed over his ruffles,
the conductor checks, inspects this
still life on his platter—
aspirin, glass; water.

The attendants will have told the crew
where it is he stands: *weltbekannt*; *begabt—*
they'll want his autograph.

He tells himself to stop.
Sip. Count. Breathe.
Ridiculous. Ridiculous.
World famous,
nevertheless whose hands thicken again

to starfish
and dessicate over a craze of notes—
black ants escaping their pages.

Rabbits at Iraklion

Peeled, vein-stringy,
strung seven across above the butcher
who throws the blade down late afternoon, town square.

He's chucking goat hooves into a bucket.
Blood runs through the table slats
and drains down into the wooden vat
for tomorrow's entrail stew.

> Stew of Judas, whose effigy's ready.
> They point and say, "Look up."
> His head is made of fruit!
> He's noosed there in the olive tree.
> His business suit flaps open—
> his spine's a splintered broom.
> His shoulder bag is crammed with silver foil.
>
> Peeled ears of lemon, and orange cheeks—
> His shoes are black wing tips, straying;
> they swing beneath his potato-made legs.
> The bell of Saint Basil's is ringing.

They'll ignite him.
Pascal candle; petrol doused from a dented can,
bang! and the black-wingèd priest, having presided,
will trail his silk sleeves to Kyria Bellisi's balcony
and spoon the Easter stew.
They'll cheer
and poke the roasted goat.

Meanwhile here the spit is being sharpened
with a screech that pulls the afternoon forward.
Our mustachioed butcher,

sweating on break,
lifts the cloudy ouzo to his mouth;
bends to untie a bleating kid for slitting and soon;
calls, "Nikos! Americans."
Sips; looks at us; grins.

IV. *Tattoo*

The angel Dumah asked her the verse that went with her name,
and when she could not answer, he split her grave with a fiery rod.

—Isaac Bashevis Singer
The Dead Fiddler

. . . your face cannot be found except veiled. But that very cloud reveals
your face to be there, beyond all veils.

—Nicholas of Cusa
The Vision of God

Tattoo

for Primo Levi

There was just the hand. There was my arm.
There was just the small pin. There was the hand.
There was my arm.

The pin's blue pinch.
The dots processing in,
some with suitcases; some with shoes.

9, the monocle of the man who dragged the pin.

2, the profile of the monocled man
who grinned and hooed with pushing the ragged pin to

6, the broken eyeglass of my father in a bloody blue.

Blue the root of this I chew again.

8, the pair of glasses I pushed through the wire for bread.

There was gunfire and then none—
Zelda, Josef, Ewa, Isaak, dead, had dug and dug:
I had to look.

Space between slashed 7 and crooked 4 traces the head of a
shovel.

Flesh layers then. The soil.

Aqua brightest vein, my ink tastes of trains,

      the tracks siphoned in and up,
      the back-to-back, the 9, the 1—

O, pulled open, mouth shouting, won't-close O, undone,
O for Oświęcim, 1943,

O, jagged on my cold old forearm—

You serpent approaching to close on itself; you fruit, bitten.

Procne

I dream of the cleaver
suspended between doors:

       Husband/Son; Son/Husband.

Nightly I am forced to choose,
and always there is the voice winding
thin as a thread of blood
through door cracks: "Mother?"

And always your laughter, Tereus,
through woodwork, assured.
How could I turn toward you?
—As though you had read it,
silver in darkness, *Itylus*
carved into the handle of that blade,
gleaming.
Waking and dreaming, I am trapped.

Look what I have done.
Rage saw me through—
it was like gutting fowl,
only he kept screaming.
Bone of bone, our flesh.

When it was finished,
I licked blood from my hands,
tasting what we'd made.

Transformed now, turned to a bird
through Mercy,
songs stall always between my heart and throat
while my sister, the one you loved,

flits between branches,
pecking cherries that are your eyes.
Recompense: her song makes poets weep.
I shed no tears but think often
of what I would have given for you.

What had you wanted all those years,
burning over me?
A son, a home, whole houses of servants
to fan your forehead;
crush grapes for you—

How we are told that our destinies are planned.
Simply: the ribbon, snipped, unrolls.

And had we to do it over again, my
Dearest, I can still see you
eyeing her through poppies;
myself bearing you whole flocks of heirs
to bleat under the slow silver flash
of wine-warm cleaver.

I Dream of the Partisans, 1941

I.

If she feels that Volodya goes, the father thinks,
she says nothing.

The peel of his apple has fallen
to the floor by his bed.
He is sitting in his socks on his bed.

It is the end of night, early December—
and snow is coming down, coming down,
beyond the papered windows of the hut.

The snow is coming down,
and now the first horse passing
which will take Ilyusha to town for sugar.

Another horse will come today, and other men.

II.

The apple is sticky in the father's big hand.
In his other hand, the cold knife.

The rest of the village is still,
but for the son who finishes his soup;
and the wind howling in the forest.

The son drinks from a clay bowl,
and one bird shrieks.

III.

The mother is looking toward the doorway.
All night she has sat in her chair.
She knows who will come.
They have not told her.
She should be doing something.
Her hair is not combed.
She keeps tugging at her sleeve.
She should say something.
Something should be done, ridiculousness!
A boy of fifteen with no good boots.

IV.

The ready boy wipes his chin.
He cleans his gun at the table and will not look up.

The snow is falling.

He skinned his own rabbits for his hat.
The hat will be warm.

The girls are asleep, two curled in their little bed.

The beds in the corner are not made, are still warm,
the son should go back to bed.
A piece of bread is left on the table;
what the son does not want.

V.

The father wants to say, Eat.
The sun will not be up for some time.

It is too dark to speak aloud.

If a father cannot speak, the father tells himself,
all the world is lost.

A Long Story

And the Lord said, 'What have you done?
The voice of your brother's blood
is crying to me from the ground . . .'
　　　　　—Genesis 4:10

It was in his own breath,
and it showed in his eyes,
and so it was
in the familiar pasture
that Cain had come to think long
of what offering was,
and he aimed.

One thought,
and something new was spent forever:
the block of offspring
broken.

Naming binds,
and *brother* was too much—
this connection to an other
through a place within the mother.
From the start it was too close.

A blue sky. Olive trees.
An ordinary day from which emerged
the rock from the boy
from the woman from the rib
from the man from the ground
from God.

Blood rushed forth from Abel's head
and mapped a path from fields

impossibly far removed
from here.

On the hands of the mother, the spilt blood.

Can you think of God—of God as a parent?
Can you think of the smoke rising around the parents,
all three?

The one child standing, *I shall be hidden,*
I shall be hidden,
in his head—
Can you think of the other child, dead?
Can you think of the hands of the mother,
the spilt blood,
and of a time
when God spoke directly to people
like someone who had been there all the while
and could not bear it?

When I stand in certain places,
the past rushes back.
I went to Warsaw and looked and looked
for Miła 18.
It was raining.

> *When we ran out of munitions,*
> *we threw bagels—*

I had a map to chart the Old.
What things can be mapped out?
Aluminum siding, a few new trees, young trees,
tennis courts, and lots

for community activities
where the buildings were razed.

No one on the streets.
One old Hasid by the Memorial selling stamps.

A bird cried out.
The wind.
Where did they all go?
A map points to things.
A cartographer may trace the physical to scale
on a piece of body, of table, of paper
if he is accurate.
I wanted accuracy. I wanted
to see it.

Just remember, renumber:
points won't correspond, but then
the theoretical becomes fact.

The house now a memory,
now an art of fiction.
I don't know I don't know I don't know.
What you pour out takes on its own life
and goes away—breath,
a body, a thought,
a prayer—
what can be owned?

Eve weeping
because again something has been taken.
Eve, the mother, with her mouth open,

and Adam turning away from the scene in the field
because he could do it, too.

Adam the father
wanting to suck them all back into himself,
and go to mud
and tell God to just start over:
maybe a more simple vessel
or a pipe.

And the reader pulling the tome from that dark shelf,
memory,
because he knows the scene to be his own
and could do it again.

Saul, Changed

I.

The voice came in my mother's own dialect
and stopped me.

There was a weaver I loved
who had a shop on a corner.
Her husband made bowls.
We could smell camels from her back room;
there were flies;
and a little curtain blew sand onto the floor.
We got sand in our mouths.

Of course she did not know
what I was really or why I came.

It was this weaver I was going to see, first,
when I heard.

II.

All of this about the steed rearing up—
the wrong things in the story
have been emphasized.
True, my horse started at the flash
but knew his course:
I had beaten him—how could he stop?

The seeing that is written of and the blindness
were part of the same course.
You could say that I realized my blindness

and despaired
because what had I done with my life?

I was thirty-four and roving,
but with decent work.
I had a strong body:
had built houses, part of a temple; some roads—
had tamed horses; could drink without being goaded to fight.
They knew my strength—
but to return to what you asked,

it was before Sabbath,
and Damascus was a carnival:
the cloth dyers had spread their bolts
over the marketplace;
the crowds were pushing to get out of the sun.

All of the water in pitchers was flashing,
and when the vendors called, "Saul—,"
how could I answer?

III.

Later, my weaver knew me still.
I was relieved—curve of her brown thigh; my changed face.
She also saw—
everything having been pushed into place.
There is room for everyone.

You might say this occurred to me for the first time
not during the light,
but during the light recalled—

I was at a fruiter's stall, and I picked out some black dates
with my right hand, some dates for my weaver.

The old fruit seller feared me,
I saw it: something hiding in him.
He dragged out a sack of the sweetest
because he feared I was not pleased.
Or perhaps he sensed my mission.

Faith

The Greek man guiding his mule through oregano,
hitting the small snakes with his stick, the Greek man
who lights the red lamps twice a day
at the top of Monemvasia because they must stay lit
is one of her incarnations.

She has been tatting for a long time.
Her blue lace is the dream web.
She has the spider's watching
and knows what you have done.
She sees your possibilities.

Faith ghostwrote Revelations 3:8
when the gods were sleeping:

> *Behold I have set before you*
> *an open door—*

Her birthday is in September.
She is the night nurse in soundless shoes,
monitoring your breathing—
clear-eyed, of no illusion;
with magnificent indigo wings.

She sees to the bottom of the cistern.
She looks into the blinding light
and proceeds.

The one blue violet
in the whole purple lawn
belongs to Faith alone,
who is irresistible.

Try to ignore her.

It is Faith who mourns, *Wait!*
from the threshold of the other world
and wraps around the near-suicide
her bluest wishes. I know this.

Once with the sweetest singing
she told me the poem was finished;
she said that I could sleep.

In the Baths, in Budapest

—1984

I.

Goulash and cream puffs for days now,
we can't bear taking our clothes off,
but decide to go—walk the crooked path
from Elesha's cramped flat in Ludvaj 14
to ascend the frosted staircase
inside the big tart.

Fountains, chandeliers,
the West Germans in leather;
a bellhop in red carries *Le Monde*
and grins passing, white-gloved.
"Sell jeans?"
He points the way, then disappears.

II.

In the first room we're given swimsuits.
Alabaster nymphs run with moisture
round this ballroom-turned-poolside—
under hanging ferns,
over marble tables, amidst unstoppered bottles
of perfume and oils.
Strauss waltzes unspool here.

Whitest tile; water blued by the lapis
of pool-floor mosaics.

We follow the older empire ladies
in their pastel turbans and heavy necklaces
and wade in.

I'm floating.
The chandeliers could close over me;
crush me slowly under.
This delicious water—
I would not fight.
My last sight, off-white sculpted cherubs
tugging carved ribbons cross-ceiling.
Sarah and Cathy, cross-pool, splashing.

III.

Slap. Stretch. Six hands then in the second room,
where I am peeled of my bathing suit
and guided through an archway.
There is steam ahead. I smell flowery oils
and hear low languages I don't know.

A cello. The trickling of water.
Hot tiles underfoot lead to a wrought iron stairway
into warm water,
and across from me in two's and three's
the women are naked, talking quietly,
some stirring the water, some floating.

I descend—green marble pool floor;
music more muted now.
Wet to the waist, I near them;

must reach them. Go under.
Push forward.

My hair drags behind.
I open my eyes to the blur of pale bodies,
one older woman with a tattoo,
blue-green, smeary on her forearm.

When I come up,
we smile at each other.
They're so wrinkled, I am thinking,
when another woman points to my abdomen
and then to the scars of her own,
saying, perhaps in Croatian:

> *Today you don't get butchered.*

Another woman takes my hand—
presses it along her gallbladder line,
under her right rib, around to her back:
it is hacked over here and there, railroad-tracked,
and I am thinking, Not that,
when yet another woman fits her hard hand
across my hipbone and says,

> *I was small the same as you,*
> *you watch, you want children, oy.*

I do not say now that I want the midwife to unzip me
when the surgeon shifts his knife,
that's all, I don't want the squall,
the giving over of life to life;
I want my own life.

IV.

It's time to go, I say,
but I don't mean it, seeing Sarah and Cathy,
and seeing myself thirty years from now,
jagged with incisions.
We're so wrinkled.
I go under.

When I open my eyes, all whites
of legs and feet waver.
Boom of my slow heart, push, pull,
the distant Strauss untunes,
I'm ragged coming up,
Eva and I tell each other our names,
all we understand out loud
until she shows me her tattoo
and says: "Baden-Baden."
The seven in the middle of the sequence
is slashed through.

V.

I have entrusted myself to three burly attendants.
One is holding a pomander.
I am helped onto a long table
and laid out face down.
Rub, rub.
Palms as big as feet, and I am flipped over,
worked over, hands and hands—
Beyond the broad pink faces above me,
the blues of the stained glass are wet with humidity.

I have a dream of my firstborn,
a big ruby extracted from my flat navel—
and water drips
from the sinuous and flowering plants in sweating pots
as these women go on in tongues
I feel I can understand.

I want just to lie here,
finished off; floating off.
Someone has draped me in the whitest, softest robe;
taken me to this *salle d'attente*
where Chopin is playing.

The others come through, and now
who is not beautiful,
the dragging breasts,
the crooked feet,
Behold.

VI.

I am handed a glass of tea in a silver filigree holder.
The woman steeps my feet in a big basin
and traces my eyebrows over and over.
She takes a gold comb to my wet hair
and hums in a low minor key.
She is all bread and garlic, and this
must be paradise, these wet leaves,
this heavy tea glass, these heavy shapes
that are other women dressing,
the alabaster heavy statues,
the heavy chandeliers,

the pieces of palaces going under,
tumbling into the heavy weight
of the heavy thing I zip shut for now
and cannot help but let deepen.

Notes

I.

"Ars Poetica": See Lorenzo de' Medici, *Opere* (Bigi/Cavalli); also John Thiem, *Selected Poems and Prose of Lorenzo de' Medici* (University Park, Pennsylvania: Pennsylvania State University Press, 1991).

ne gli occhi hanno altro lume che l'obietto / neither do the eyes have any other light but the object
poi ch'io gustai . . . la tua dolcezza / because I have tasted your sweetness

"The Kyria's Tuesday Vigil":

Kyria / Mrs.

"Riddles":

swiving / from the Old English (Anglo-Saxon) *swifan* (to rut)

"At the Raptor Center":

Antinöus (110–130) was the emperor Hadrian's lover whose beauty was legendary. When Antinöus drowned under mysterious circumstances, Hadrian declared him deified and founded the Egyptian city of Antinöopolis in his honor.

"Cleopatra at the Mirror": This poem was inspired by Acts II and V of Shakespeare's play. The villanelle form in particular was inspired by Act II.v—"Let him not leave out the colour of her hair," and "I am pale, Charmian."

Cydnus / the Nile
mandragora / a narcotic
Worm of Nilus / the asp (V. 2)

II.

Czesław Miłosz, *The Collected Poems* (New York: The Ecco Press, 1988).

"From Bourbonnais": This poem refers to the Second Crusade (1145–1149).

"In the Attic": The epigraph is from Justin O'Brien's translation of Albert Camus' *The Fall* (New York: Knopf, 1966). *"La terre est obscure . . ."* (Part II) is from Albert Camus' *La Chute*. *"Für Dich, für Dich . . ."* (Part IV) lines are from Heinrich Heine, *Lyrik*. "Magritte's *Gigantesques*" (Part V) refers to *Les jours gigantesques* in Brussels. See also A. M. Hammacher, trans. James Brockway, *Magritte* (New York: Harry N. Abrams, Inc., no date). Phrasing in Part VI ("Debauchery . . . immortality" and "is liberated . . . hope") is a deliberate reference and homage to Justin O'Brien's translation of Camus' *The Fall* (New York: Knopf, 1966).

Hol' mir die Flasche ein! / Get me the bottle!
Kannst Du aber spüren / Can you at all feel how I love you?
Ob Du mich noch liebst? / (I asked) if you love me; if you still love me.
Ohne Zweifel / Without a doubt
Schau' mal aus dem Fenster hinaus! / Look out the window!
La terre est obscure, chère amoure / The earth is dark, dear love,
le bois épais, opaque le linceul! / the coffin thick; the shroud opaque!
Hol' mir die Flasche! / Get me the bottle!
Blauestes Röschen / Bluest little rose
Für Dich, für Dich, / For you, for you,
Es hat mein Herz für Dich geschlagen— / My heart has beaten for you.

"Whatever the White Mountain Means":

Wasatch / the Wasatch Range of the Rocky Mountains

III.

"Melancholia, Five Movements":

Für die Mutter Gottes / for the mother of God

"Our Lady of Częstochowa" refers to a medieval Polish painting of the Madonna that was slashed in 1430 during a battle. Since the late Middle Ages the damaged painting has been the center of a shrine celebrated for its miraculous healings at Jasna Góra near Kraków.

"Veronica and the Strange Cloth": Veronica Wipes the Face of Jesus, the Sixth Station of the Cross i the Roman Catholic tradition, is a meditation on compassion. In the fourteenth century the story o compassionate woman offering her veil to Christ on his way to Calvary became popular.

"Tuesday the Conductor Travels":

weltbekannt / world famous
begabt / talented

"Rabbits At Iraklion": In parts of Crete and the Peloponnese it is the custom to hang and explode a effigy of Judas on Easter Sunday.

IV.

Isaac Bashevis Singer, "The Dead Fiddler," in *The Collected Stories* (New York: Farrar Strauss Giroux, 1982).

"Tattoo":

Oświęcim / Auschwitz

"Procne": According to Greek mythology, Procne killed her son, Itylus, and fed him to her husband, Tereus, after learning that Tereus had raped and ripped out the tongue of Philomel, Procne's sister.

Through the intercession of the gods, Procne and Philomel, pursued by Tereus, were turned respectively into a swallow and a nightingale.

"I Dream of the Partisans, 1941": This poem was inspired by Elem Klimov's brilliant film, *Come and See* (1985) and is dedicated to the memory of Volodya Shcherbatsevich, 15-year-old resistance member hanged by the Nazis in 1941, and to my brothers, JMS and JGS.

"A Long Story": Miła 18 was the headquarters of the Warsaw Ghetto Uprising.

"In the Baths, in Budapest": This poem is for my dear friends, Catherine L. Mackenzie, RN, and Sarah T. Borwein, MD.